The Amazing Milk Book

Written by

Catherine Ross

and

Susan Wallace

Illustrated by

Linda Hendry

D1214843

Addison-Wesley Publishing Company, Inc.

Reading, Massachusetts   Menlo Park, California   New York
Don Mills, Ontario   Wokingham, England   Amsterdam   Bonn
Sydney   Singapore   Tokyo   Madrid   San Juan
Paris   Seoul   Milan   Mexico City   Taipei

Many of the designations used by manufacturers and sellers to distinguish their products are claimed as trademarks. Where those designations appear in this book and Addison-Wesley was aware of a trademark claim, the designations have been printed in initial capital letters (i.e., Styrofoam).

Neither the Publisher nor the author shall be liable for any damage which may be caused or sustained as a result of the conduct of any of the activities in this book.

Library of Congress Cataloging-in-Publication Data
Ross, Catherine Sheldrick.
    The amazing milk book / Catherine Sheldrick Ross and Susan Wallace ; illustrations by Linda Hendry
        p.   cm.
    "Originally published in Canada by Kids Can Press, Ltd., of Toronto, Ontario"—T.p. verso.
    Includes index.
    Summary: Describes the content of milk, where it comes from, its various uses, and how it gets from cow to carton.
    ISBN 0-201-57087-4
    1. Milk—Juvenile literature.   2. Dairying—Juvenile literature.
[1. Milk. 2. Dairying.] I. Wallace, Susan, 1946–   II. Hendry, Linda, ill. III. Title.
SF239.5.R67   1991
637'.1—dc20   90-49636
                                                         CIP
                                                         AC

Originally published in Canada by Kids Can Press, Ltd., of Toronto, Ontario.

Edited by Laurie Wark and Valerie Wyatt
Interior designed by Michael Solomon
Set in 12-point Primer by Alphabets

1 2 3 4 5 6 7 8 9-VB-9594939291
First printing, February 1991

Other Books in this Activity Series

Acknowledgements

Many people helped out with this book and we would like to thank them now. Gail Ewan, director of Nutrition Information, and her staff at the Dairy Bureau of Canada gave us invaluable help with the nutritional aspects of milk and dairy products. Various people involved in the Agriculture in the Classroom program (sponsored by the Ontario Ministry of Agriculture and Food) — consultants, dairy farmers, a nutritionist and a veterinarian — set us straight on the farming aspects of milk production. Our thanks to Ruth Behnke and the Learning Materials Committee of the Agriculture in the Classroom program for reviewing the manuscript and providing helpful suggestions. We also want to acknowledge the information provided by the Ontario Milk Marketing Board, the Holland Cheese Exporters Association, the Dairy Farmers of Canada and the American Dairy Products Institute. The cheesemaker at the Blanchard and Nissouri Cheese Company helped by providing a tour of a cheesemaking operation. Thanks are also due to Dr. Patricia Blackshaw for medical advice and to Murray Ross for advice on chemical reactions. We thank the students in Catherine Ross's course on Reference at the School of Library and Information Science at the University of Western Ontario who tracked down elusive facts about baby whales as milk drinkers. Our children, Elizabeth, Jacob and Sarah, helped test the material, gave moral support but didn't do any of the typing of the manuscript. And finally we are indebted to our editors, Val Wyatt and Laurie Wark, whose editing skills and generous encouragement were invaluable.

Contents

*I*MAGINE a world without milk. You get up for breakfast and pour yourself a bowl of cereal. Try eating it without milk. Make some toast. How does it taste without butter? Without milk and food made from milk, breakfast can be ho-hum. The rest of your day would be pretty tasteless without milk, too. Forget about eggnog, strawberry yogurt, ice-cream cones and milk shakes, and say good-bye to puddings and pancakes. They're all made with milk.

Milk is special. It's the first food you eat. It's so good for you that you can live on nothing but milk for at least the first six months of your life. Milk is one of two substances in the world whose sole purpose is to be a food. (The other is honey.)

Apples, corn, eggs — they're all good to eat, but they weren't made to be eaten. Their purpose is to create new apple trees or new corn plants or baby chickens. But the *only* purpose of milk is to feed baby animals. That's why it's the most complete single food there is.

In this book you'll read about some amazing milk makers and milk drinkers; learn how milk can be made into paint and glue; try out some delicious milk recipes; make some milk-carton crafts; and even discover what food you should feed to dragons to calm them down when they are angry.

Whenever you see a milk word that you don't understand, check the glossary at the back of the book.

1. Magic milk & cow tales

Because milk is such an essential food, people from very early times have told many stories about it. Milk is often presented as a magical substance that can give youth, health, even life itself. In some stories, taking a bath in milk cures a sick person or heals an injured person's wounds.

Cleopatra, Queen of Egypt, used to bathe in donkey's milk to stay young-looking.

One myth says that, after their death, people go to a land that flows with rivers of milk, wine, oil and honey. In a story told in India, milk flows not just in rivers but in oceans. The Indian god Rama churned an ocean of milk and produced the potion of life.

In western Europe, people used to leave out saucers of milk for the house spirits to drink. They believed that this would keep the house safe and protected them from bad spirits.

The tomb of the ancient Egyptian god Osiris was surrounded by 365 tables, one table for each day of the year. According to the story, every morning the god drank the offering of milk put on the table and was brought back to life.

On St. George's Day (April 23), French and German peasants used to put wreaths of flowers on their cows' heads to ensure lots of milk for the coming season.

Romulus

and Remus

According to legend, twin baby boys called Romulus and Remus were born to the god Mars in ancient Rome Their uncle Amulius was a cruel king who had seized power. He feared these twins because they were the true heirs to the throne and so he decided to kill them. On his orders, the babies were put in a basket and thrown into the Tiber River. The basket floated downstream and finally came to shore safely. The murder plot was spoiled by a wolf, who found the twins and took pity on them.

She raised them, along with her own wolf-cubs, and fed them her milk.

It turned out that the uncle was right to fear Romulus and Remus. When they grew up and found out who they really were, they killed him. Then, according to the legend, in 753 BC they established a city right on the spot where they had been rescued from the Tiber River by the wolf. This became the great city of Rome, named after Romulus.

Some people used to believe that if you drank milk, you would become like the animal who had produced the milk. If you drank donkey or camel milk, for example, you might become stubborn, just like those animals. So people thought that the wolf milk that Romulus and Remus drank as babies made them wolf-like conquerors. What about us cow's-milk drinkers — what qualities do you think drinking cow's milk might give us?

It makes us a-moo-sing?
We become Bossy?
It turns us into cow-ards?
We don't like to moo-ve around too much?

Survival Hint:
It may come in handy sometime to know that, according to folk tales, you can feed milk to a dragon to keep it quiet.

Don't just drink your milk. Write with it!

Here's how to make invisible messages. Only friends who know your secret will be able to read what you have written.

You'll need:
  an old straight pen (the kind where you put a nib into a wooden penholder). A fountain pen or even a large feather will also work.
  milk
  unlined white paper
  a lamp

1. Dip the nib of your pen (or the tip of your feather) into the milk. Carefully print your message on paper. Don't press too hard, and don't use too much milk.
2. Let the milk dry on the paper until your message has disappeared. This may take an hour.

3. Your friend can make your words come to light by turning on a lamp and holding the paper over the light bulb (not too close though; you don't want to burn the paper).

How does it work?
All milk contains protein. The heat from the light bulb causes the protein in the milk to burn. When the protein burns, it turns from white to brown, revealing your words.

More cow tales

A hot time in the old town tonight

Remember the camper's song?

One dark night when we were all in bed,
Mother O'Leary left the lantern in the shed.
And when the cow kicked it over, she
   winked one eye and said,
"There'll be a hot time in the old town
   tonight."
Fire! Fire! Fire!

There are no witnesses, but legend has it
that Mrs. O'Leary's cow gave a full pail of
milk. Then, being ornery, the cow kicked
over a lantern and started a fire in the
barn. This became the great Chicago fire
of October 10, 1871. No wonder Mrs.
O'Leary's cow has been immortalized in
song. This fire was one of the greatest
disasters in American history. It destroyed
almost the entire city of Chicago, burned
down 17 500 buildings, killed several hundred people and put 90 000 people out of
their homes. Quite an impact for one
cow's kick!

Cow double agent

You may have heard of Laura Secord's chocolates, but what about her cow? According to legend, Laura Secord used her cow as a cover story for a secret mission during the only war ever fought between Canada and the United States. In 1812, Great Britain was fighting a war in Europe against France. The U.S. declared war on Britain and attacked Canada, which then belonged to Britain. Most of the battles of the War of 1812-14 were fought along the border area of the Great Lakes, especially near Buffalo and in the Niagara Falls area. The story is told that Laura Secord and her cow made a heroic journey through the bush near Niagara Falls to warn the British of an American attack.

What really happened? In June 1813, Laura Secord walked a roundabout route of 32 km (20 miles) through woods and fields to warn Lieutenant James Fitzgibbon of a coming attack; with this information, he was able to defeat the American force. Laura Secord didn't get public recognition for her heroic walk for another 47 years; by then, she was 85 years old. But after 1860, poems and plays were written about her, and the story got better every time it was told. A book published in 1864 apparently invented the detail that Laura Secord brought along a cow on her walk as a cover-up and milked it right under the noses of American sentries.

In memory of a super cow

In Woodstock, Ontario, there is a larger-than-life statue of a black and white Holstein-Friesian cow. It was put there to honour Springbank Snow Countess (born November 18, 1919, and died August 9, 1936), who was a "world champion lifetime butterfat producer." She produced 3656 kg (8062 lbs) of milk fat and 94 122 kg (207 500 lbs) of milk in ten lactations (a lactation is the ten-month period each year that a cow is milked). These days, cows have to do better than that, however. According to the *Guinness Book of World Records*, the record for the greatest lifetime yield of cow's milk was set by a Holstein-Friesian from California with the unglamorous name of No. 289. She produced 211 025 kg (465 224 lbs) of milk before she died in 1984.

2.
So, what is milk?

You may have heard, "Drink up all your milk" more often than, "Finish up all your soda pop." Soda pop is mostly water, with some added sugar and flavourings. Cow's milk is mostly water, too — 87% — which is why it's such a good thirst quencher. But it's the other 13% of milk that makes cow's milk better for you than soda pop; this part of the milk is called milk solids and contains 55 essential nutrients.

What's milk made of?

The composition of cow's milk varies a bit, from one cow to another and from one breed to another. Three substances that aren't found in any other food give milk its remarkable qualities: milk sugar, milk fat and milk protein.

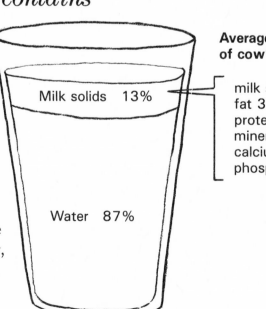

Milk solids   13%

Water   87%

Average composition of cow's milk

milk sugar   5%
fat 3.8%
protein   3.5%
minerals (such as calcium and phosphorus)   .7%

Milk sugar, or lactose, is the ingredient in milk that allows it to ferment or sour. Lactose is only one-quarter as sweet as the sugar in your sugar-bowl, but certain kinds of bacteria like it that way. These bacteria digest some of the lactose in milk and turn it into the acid that gives sour cream and yogurt their sour taste.

Milk fat is the rich-tasting ingredient that butter, whipping cream and ice cream are made from. The fat is in the form of spherical globules that are dispersed throughout the milk. These fat globules can clump together into larger particles, which is what happens when butter is made. The fat globules don't stick together easily, however, because each globule is wrapped in a protein coating, or

membrane. When you churn butter or whip cream, you are doing all that work to break down the fat globule membranes.

Milk protein is the ingredient in milk that coagulates to form solid curds. Casein, which makes up 80% of the protein, turns into curds when cheese is made (the word casein comes from the Latin word *caseus*, which means cheese). Whey proteins make up the other 20% of milk protein.

A drop of milk up close

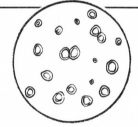

Up close, milk doesn't look like milk at all! When you look at a drop of milk under a microscope, you see a transparent, or see-through, liquid with many different-sized particles floating in it. These particles are globules of fat surrounded with a coating of casein protein, and there are about 100 million of them in every drop of milk.

You can't see the lactose or the protein in the magnified milk drop. Units of lactose and protein are too small to see,

even with a microscope. Casein particles are about 400 times smaller than fat globules, and units of lactose are even smaller.

Why can't you see through milk? Because lightwaves can't pass straight through milk, the way they pass through water. When light hits your glass of milk, it bounces off fat globules and other tinier particles, and the lightwaves scatter. This refraction of light is what makes milk white. Some milk is whiter than others, because the whiteness of milk depends on the number and the size of the particles suspended in the milk. Skim milk has a bluish colour.

Solutions, suspensions and emulsions

An ordinary glass of milk might not look very complex to you. But to a chemist, it's a glass containing lactose in solution as well as tiny bundles of casein proteins in colloidal suspension, not to mention fat globules in emulsion. What?

We know that milk contains fat globules and particles of lactose and proteins. The size and kind of particles determines whether you have a true **solution**, a **suspension** or an **emulsion**. In a true solution, molecules (or particles) dissolve in the liquid. In a suspension, larger clusters of molecules are dispersed, or evenly distributed, in the liquid — just hanging there. And in an emulsion, globules of one kind of liquid are dispersed in another liquid.

Experiment by making a solution yourself. Stir a spoonful of sugar into a glass of water. When the sugar disappears so that the liquid is clear, you have a true solution. (With a solution, you can hold a book behind a glass of the substance and read the words right through the solution.) Dip your finger into your solution and taste it. The sugar is still there, even if you can't see it. No matter how long you wait, the sugar won't drop to the bottom of the glass. Molecules of lactose are dissolved in milk the same way that sugar dissolved in your glass of water.

Next make a suspension. Take a glass of milk and mix some chocolate powder into

it. Those brown chocolate particles are suspended in your glass of milk, but they can come out again. If you pour your chocolate milk through a coffee filter paper, you see chocolate powder left behind on the filter. (A sugar solution would pass right through and leave nothing behind.) Mud in water and dust in air are two other kinds of suspensions. You can see a suspension of dust in air when light shines through the window on a sunny day.

You can make an emulsion that you can eat afterwards — an oil-and-vinegar salad dressing. First find a glass jar that has a tight-fitting lid. Pour some vegetable oil and some vinegar into the jar — 4 parts oil to every 1 part vinegar. Look at the two liquids in the jar. Can you see which is oil and which is vinegar? Now screw the top securely on the jar and shake hard. Presto — an emulsion. Emulsions tend to separate. That's why you have to shake up dressing just before tossing it with your salad. Emulsions stay mixed better when there is an emulsifying agent. The emulsifying agent that helps keep milk fat suspended in milk is casein, which coats the fat globule.

Milk explosions

You can make milk explode into action just by adding detergent. If you add food colouring to the milk, you can watch while you create a small tempest in your teacup.

You'll need:
  milk
  a bowl (or a big teacup)
  at least two colours of food
    colouring
  liquid dish detergent
  a toothpick

1. Pour enough milk into your bowl to cover the bottom.
2. Carefully add to the milk a drop of each of your colours of food colouring. Keep the drops as far away from each other as possible.

3. Put a drop of detergent on the tip of a toothpick and touch it to the food colouring.
4. Watch the fire works! No noise, but lots of lovely swirls of colour.

How does it work?
The effect of detergent on the surface tension of milk causes this explosion of colour. When you touched the surface of the milk with detergent, you weakened its surface tension at that spot, causing a ripple to explode outward and mix up the food colouring. What colour have you ended up with? Try using different colour combinations.

Make Miss Muffet's curds and whey

Did you know that when Little Miss Muffet sat on a tuffet, eating her curds and whey, she was really eating curdled milk? It was like cottage cheese, only wetter and more sour. You can make your own curds and whey. You may even be able to tempt a spider to sit down beside you while you eat them.

You'll need:
> 500 mL (2 cups) of milk (You can make Milk Glue on the next page if you use skim milk here. Milk containing milk fat would make greasy glue.)
> a saucepan
> 50 mL (3 tbsp) of vinegar or lemon juice
> a wooden spoon
> a bowl

1. Pour the milk into the saucepan. Add the vinegar or lemon juice.
2. Put the saucepan on low heat and stir slowly until the milk curdles (makes curds) — about eight minutes.
3. Remove the saucepan from the heat but keep stirring until all the curdling stops. You will see solids (the curd) and liquid (the whey).
4. Put the mixture in a bowl and refrigerate. When the curds and whey are cool, they will be ready to eat. Taste them. Add salt or sugar, if you like.

How does it work?
When milk separates into curds and whey, we say that it has curdled or "coagulated." How does this happen? When you add an acid like vinegar or lemon juice to milk, you change the shape of the casein. In its changed shape, casein clumps together, or coagulates, to form solid curds. Heat helps separate the curds from the liquid whey. (Another thing that makes milk coagulate is an enzyme called rennet, which is made from the stomachs of nursing calves.)

Curd contains most of the fat, casein protein and vitamin A of the original milk. But whey has important nutrients, too. Whey is 93% water, but it also contains whey proteins, some minerals and vitamins, and most of the lactose of the original milk. In North America, dehydrating the whey left over from the cheesemaking process is big business. Dried whey is sold as a nutritious additive for bread, ice cream, processed luncheon meats and even food for animals.

Milk glue

You can make glue out of milk curds — the same white glue that you use to glue paper. Here's how to make your own milk glue.

You'll need:
  milk curds (follow the instructions on the previous page for making Miss Muffet's curds and whey)
  a colander
  paper towels
  a mixing bowl
  60 mL (¼ cup) water   2 Tbs.
  15 mL (1 tbsp) baking soda
  a wooden spoon
  a plastic yogurt cup with a lid

1. Pour the curds and whey through a colander lined with a paper towel.
2. Blot the curds dry with a paper towel.

3. Put the curds into a mixing bowl.
4. Add the water and the baking soda to the curds in the bowl and stir. You should see some tiny bubbles. Beat until the mixture is smooth.

5. Store your glue in the fridge in a yogurt cup with a lid so that the glue doesn't dry out.

If you think that white glue is too boring, add food colouring. Try out the strength of your glue by pasting together two pieces of paper. Let the glue dry and then try to separate the paper.

Casein is remarkable stuff. Simple milk curds, like the ones you just made, can be combined with chemicals and then hardened into plastics. Casein is used to make combs, jewellery, even some house paints. Casein glue in paint is what makes it stick to your walls and ceilings. Casein has been made into fibre for clothing, too.

What's in it for you?

Fat makes your hair shine, gives you energy and contains vitamins. Vitamin A helps you see in the dark and helps your body fight infection.

Calcium, a mineral, makes your teeth strong and healthy.

Calcium builds strong bones. Calcium is also needed whenever your muscles contract, and it helps clot the blood when you get a cut, so that you stop bleeding.

Milk protein builds and repairs muscles and other body tissues.

Riboflavin is a B vitamin needed for your nervous system and for growth.

Lactose, or milk sugar, gives you energy.

The Recommended Daily Allowance of milk is two to four servings each day, depending on your age. One serving is 250 mL (1 cup) of milk or its equivalent in cheese, ice cream or yogurt.

Test your nutrition smarts

Next time you eat your breakfast cereal, look at the box. What does it say? That Super-Frosted Chocolate Sugar Bits are a good dietary source of protein when taken with 125 mL (½ cup) of milk?

So which of the following do you think would be "a good dietary source of protein" when taken with milk?

(a) 1 serving of breakfast cereal
(b) 125 mL (½ cup) of sawdust
(c) 1 mushroom
(d) 10 potato chips

The answer is that *all* of the above are good sources of protein when eaten with milk. The protein is in the milk — 4.5 grams in each 125 mL (½ cup) serving. We don't recommend the sawdust-and-milk treat, though, even if it does have protein.

Find the hidden milk

How much milk do you eat in a day? On a piece of paper, keep a list of what you eat in a day. Don't forget the snacks: the milk and peanut-butter cookie after school and the chocolate pudding at recess. Was there butter on the bread in your sandwich? Write that down, too.

Look at your list and count up how much milk you've eaten. It's not too hard to keep track of the glasses of milk you drank. But what about the hidden milk that you ate? Cheese, yogurt, sour cream, butter, ice cream and sherbet are foods made from milk. So are mashed potatoes, cream soup, pudding, pancakes, muffins, doughnuts and milk chocolate candy. Take a look at the list of ingredients on a package of crunchy granola, crackers, cookies and cake mixes. See if the ingredients include "milk solids" or "skim milk powder" or "whey powder." These are all dried forms of milk. Even sausages often contain "milk fillers."

Ask Doctor Pat

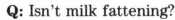

Have you ever heard milk called bone food? Or wondered why some people can't drink milk? If you want to know more about how healthy milk is, ask Doctor Pat; she's a family doctor.

Q: Is milk always good for you? Why is it that some people can't drink milk?

Dr. Pat: Milk *can* make some people sick, especially adults. Babies all drink milk as their first food. But many people lose their ability to digest milk. Why? In order to digest milk, people must produce lactase. Lactase is an enzyme that is needed to process the lactose or milk sugar found in milk. Most adults from Europe and their descendants continue to produce lactase, and so have no problem digesting milk. But some people from countries that don't have a dairy tradition, such as China, Japan and parts of Africa, stop producing enough lactase and may suffer from "lactose intolerance." For these people, milk may be a big pain in the gut.

People who can't digest lactose in a glass of milk may also have trouble eating ice cream, milk puddings and milk-based soups.

Q: Isn't milk fattening?

Dr. Pat: Not unless you eat more of it — and of other foods, too — than your body needs for energy. Energy in food is measured in calories or kilojoules. A 250-mL (1-cup) serving of whole milk contains 660 kJ (160 calories) — about the same as two eggs or seven gumdrops. If you weigh 45 kg (100 lbs), one cup of whole milk gives you the energy to skip for 17 minutes, bicycle for 22 minutes, swim for 27 minutes, hike for 30 minutes, skate for 41 minutes or play a computer game for 100 minutes.

When we say a food is fattening, we mean it has a lot of calories in proportion to the other nutrients it provides. A glass of whole milk would give you about the same number of calories as 15 potato chips. But when you eat potato chips, all you get is calories and a craving for more. The glass of milk, on the other hand, provides average 10-to-12-year-old kids with about one-fifth of their daily protein needs — and many vitamins and minerals besides.

Q: My parents call milk "bone food." How come?

Dr. Pat: Your bones and teeth are made out of calcium — in fact, 99% of the calcium in your body is in your teeth and bones in the form of calcium phosphate. Since bones completely replace themselves every seven years, we need to get a lot of calcium from the foods we eat to replace the calcium in our bones. In the United States and Canada, about 75% of the calcium we get comes from milk and milk products.

Bones also need vitamin D. Without it, children may develop rickets, a condition that weakens the leg bones so much that the legs become bowed. In North America and some parts of Europe, vitamin D is added in tiny quantities to milk. An adult can get all the vitamin D needed in 250 mL (1 cup) of milk a day. Babies under two years old need four times that much milk to get their daily dose of vitamin D. Of course, you can always get your vitamin D from cod liver oil, if you'd rather — or from lots of sunshine.

3. Where does milk come from?

What do you have in common with the duck-billed platypus, the whale, the mouse and the kangaroo? You're all milk drinkers. There are about 4000 different species of animals who feed their young milk. They are called mammals — nature's only milk producers.

Milk production is the only feature that distinguishes mammals from all other backboned animals, such as birds or amphibians. Mammals get their name from the mammary glands, where the milk is made. When a mother mammal has given birth, her mammary glands begin to produce milk. Mammary glands occur in pairs. A mother who usually produces only one baby at a time, such as a whale or a monkey or a bat, has just one pair of mammary glands. But tenrecs, hedgehog-like creatures from the island of Madagascar, have 11 pairs of mammary glands to feed as many as 20 babies at a time.

Most baby mammals start to nurse right after they are born. Even newborn mice or kittens, who are so helpless at birth that they cannot see or hear or hold up their heads, can still push themselves towards their mother's teat (the nipple on the mammary gland) and begin to feed.

Teats are found in different places on different animals' bodies. Mother elephants have a pair of teats between their front legs. Mother bats have a pair between their wings. Deer, cows, horses and goats have teats between their hind legs. Kangaroos have them inside their pouches. Pigs have many pairs of teats that extend the whole length of the belly to feed their large litters. The duck-billed platypus and the echidna from Australia, New Guinea and Tasmania have no teats at all. Their milk oozes like sweat through pores and onto the skin for the baby to lap up.

Some baby animals can go longer between meals than others. Baby mice suckle every 20 minutes, piglets every hour, rabbits once a day and tree shrews once every two days.

How do the mammary glands know how much milk to produce? Do twins have to order ahead for extra rations? Luckily, the milk supply quickly adjusts to the demand. The more milk the babies drink, the more milk is produced. Sucking on the teat stimulates the glands that produce milk. When the babies stop sucking, the mammary glands stop getting the signal that makes them produce milk.

The mammary gland

Milk is made in milk-secreting cells that are found in the alveoli. As shown in this diagram of a human breast, the alveoli are arranged like grapes on a stem, joined by a duct system. Milk drains from

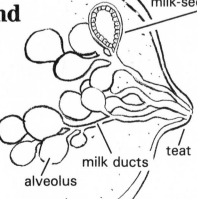

milk-secreting cells

alveolus

milk ducts

teat

the alveoli through small ducts into larger ducts. In cows, these large ducts empty their milk into four large containers or cisterns in the udder. At milking time, the milk comes out through a single hole in the teat.

Amazing milk drinkers

The biggest

Some blue whale babies drink as much as 600 L (132 gallons) of milk a day, and they do their drinking underwater. Whales breathe air just as we do, so they have to gulp down a lot of milk at one time before going to the surface for more air. Their mothers help them out by using special muscles in their mammary glands to squeeze huge streams of milk into the baby's mouth. All the babies have to do is open their mouths and swallow. On a steady diet of milk, a baby blue whale can gain 90 kg (200 lbs) a day. That's more than most adult people weigh!

The longest

Polar bear mothers nurse their babies the longest for any animal their size — up to two years. Yet for several months of the year these moms eat almost nothing but berries.

The smallest

This common long-eared bat is one of the smallest mammals known — it weighs less than 15 g (0.5 oz). The endangered Kitti's hog-nosed bat of Thailand is even smaller. It's no bigger than a bumblebee and weighs about as much as a penny. Bat babies drink their milk upside-down, since their mothers rest by hanging suspended by their toes.

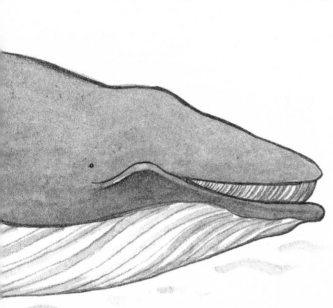

Quit pushing

Since a mother pig sometimes has 18 or 20 babies in one litter, she has to be able to nurse a lot of them at once. She lies down on her side so that the piglets can nurse from her two rows of teats. Some piglets stand on the backs of the others — like bunk beds or a double-decker bus.

I'm stuck in this pocket!

At birth, a kangaroo baby is not even as long as your little finger. As soon as it's born, it wriggles into its mother's pouch to find a teat. The mother's teat then swells until it gets stuck in the baby's mouth. This arrangement makes it easy for the mother kangaroo to pump milk into her baby's mouth. When the baby gets bigger, its jaws can open wide enough to let go of the teat. At nine months, the kangaroo baby leaves the pouch but continues to nurse until its first birthday.

Make mine chocolate

Human babies, like other mammals, drink breast milk. Milk changes to meet the baby's needs as it grows from birth to its first birthday and older. The first milk (called *colostrum*) flows for only a few days after birth and is thick and slightly yellow. Colostrum contains a strong dose of antibodies that protect the baby against infections. After a few days, breast milk becomes thin and bluish. Then, as the baby gets older, the milk changes again. Human milk may be bluish, but Jersey cow milk is yellowish and kangaroo milk is pinkish.

Milk makers for people

Which animals make milk for people to drink? If you said cows, you're partly right. People have been drinking cow's milk for a long time. A carved stone panel found by archeologists at the Temple of Ur in Babylon shows Sumerian priests in about 3500 BC milking cows and collecting the milk in large stone jars. The Sumerians were probably the first people to raise milk cows. Now, nine out of every ten glasses of milk consumed by people come from cows.

Sumerian priests milk cows in an ancient carving

But cows have won out as our chief milk producers only recently. In some parts of the world, people still get their milk from animals other than cows. Which animals? Read on to find out.

I have been called the poor man's cow. I can find food on the rocky sides of mountains where a cow would break her neck or starve. Heidi's grandfather made his cheese from my milk. Some people find my milk easier to digest than cow's milk. The fat globules in my milk are smaller than in cow's milk, and so gravity won't make my cream separate and rise to the top. (See Creamed milk, page 42)

After the cow, I produce the most milk for people. I provide half of all milk drunk in India. If you lived in India, you would also eat a liquid butter called ghee, made from my milk.

Goat

Water Buffalo

It takes two people to milk me — one to do the milking and the other to hold my horns to make me stay in one place. But if you were a Laplander from northern Scandinavia, you would probably get your milk from me, because no other dairy animal can survive in such a cold barren place. My milk has 22% fat — six times as much as cow's milk has.

Fierce Mongolian warriors who rode with Genghis Khan more than 700 years ago made a dried-out, concentrated paste from my milk. They used it as food when they were on the march. At meal time, they put this paste in water, beat it up and drank it — the world's first dried milk powder! In southeastern Russia, people still use my milk to make a fermented, slightly alcoholic drink called kumiss.

I may be the first animal milked by humans. My babies can double their birth weight in ten days on a diet of my milk, which has twice the fat content of cow's milk. My milk is used to make French Roquefort cheese, one of the most famous cheeses in the world.

Reindeer

Horse

Sheep

On the hot desert, my milk spoils much more slowly than other milk. It lasts for seven days at 30° C (86° F). In your nice cold refrigerator, it would last for three months.

In the cold mountains of Tibet, people make yak butter tea. You might think that this Tibetan favourite tastes nothing like tea. You're right; it's actually more like hot, salty, creamy soup, whipped to a froth.

Camel

Yak

Growth potion

If you think all milk is the same, you should try a glass of seal's milk. It has 12 times as much fat and four times as much protein as cow's milk. With this rich milk, it's no wonder that some seal babies can double their birth weight in six days. Human babies take about five months to double their birth weights. But if they gained weight at the rate of seal babies and kept it up for an entire

month, they would be bigger than most full-grown people by the time they were a month old!

The amazing food machine

Q: How can you turn grass into milk?
A: Feed it to a cow.

Those dairy cows you see standing in the fields with their udders full of milk are all mothers. How do we know? Because a cow will not produce any milk until she has first had a calf, which usually happens when she is two years old. (Until she is old enough to become a mother, she is called a heifer.) After her calf is born, she is milked for ten months or 205 days. Since a good cow can produce 20 times as much milk as her calf needs, there's lots left over for the farmer to sell.

Every year, each cow gets a two-month holiday. During her holiday she is not milked and therefore she stops producing milk. She rests and builds up nutrients in her body to be ready for her new baby calf, which is born every spring. Then she starts producing milk again.

A cow that is giving milk needs to eat huge amounts of grasses, corn and hay each day. The cow can digest this tough diet of cellulose because she has a large four-chambered stomach. She also eats grains and seeds such as barley, corn, oats and soybeans.

Eating and chewing take up a lot of the cow's day. But cows don't chew their food at first; they gulp it down fast. The food goes first into the largest compartment of the stomach, the *rumen* (ROO-min), where the roughage is churned,

moistened and softened. The rumen is like a big, warm fermentation vat, big enough to hold 180 L (48 gallons). It contains helpful microbes like bacteria that partially digest the food for the cow, breaking down tough plant fibres. When the food reaches the second compartment, the *reticulum* (ruh-TIC-u-lum), it is formed into lumps of partially digested grasses called cuds, which are wads about the size of tennis balls. The cow uses her stomach muscles to send the cuds one at a time back to her mouth to be rechewed.

When you see a herd of cows lying under a tree looking content, they're really quite busy chewing their cud. This chewing breaks up the tough fibres into small particles and mixes them with saliva. Cows can spend eight hours each day just chewing their cud or ''ruminating.'' (Other animals besides cattle are ruminants, too — grazing animals such as deer, buffalo, giraffes, sheep and goats. They also have four compartments in their stomach and swallow their food twice.)

When the cud is thoroughly chewed into small particles, the cow swallows it again. This time it goes on into the third compartment called the *omasum* (OH-MAY-sum) where it is softened and ground up some more. Finally the food is forced into the fourth compartment, the *abomasum* (AB-o-MAY-sum). The abomasum is sometimes called the true

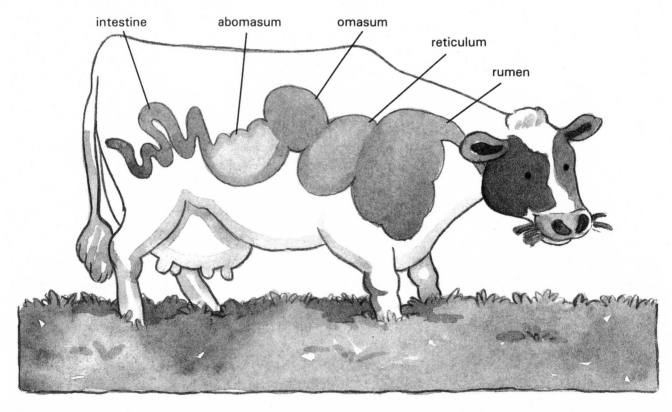

intestine   abomasum   omasum   reticulum   rumen

stomach, because it works the same way your stomach does. Here, acids further digest the food.

The digested food passes into the small intestine where digestion is completed and the nutrients are absorbed into the blood. A lot of these nutrients are carried by the blood to the udder.

How is milk removed from a full udder? One way is to use a calf, which grasps the teat with its tongue and presses out the milk against the roof of its mouth. Another way — the way our pioneer ancestors did it — is to milk the cow by hand. These days most farmers have large herds of cows and use milking machines, which is a lot quicker and more sanitary. A milking machine takes only about five minutes to milk a cow and can milk several cows at once. (See More Milk, p. 41)

Farmers milk their cows twice a day, usually in the morning and evening, at the same times each day. Cows like routine in their life, not surprises. When a cow is ready for milking, she lets people know by making a deep, mooing noise called lowing. Cows can be very noisy and demanding until they are milked!

The cow is an amazingly efficient milk factory. It takes her only about 50 to 70 hours to turn green grass into white milk.

Big eaters

A typical dairy cow eats tons of food each year. Every day she consumes:

a bathtub full of water (60 L [or 67 quarts])

4 kg (9 lbs) of haylage, or fermented chopped hay

16 kg (36 lbs) of silage, which is the whole corn plant, chopped and fermented

4 kg (9 lbs) of mixed grains and processed concentrated feeds containing salt, other minerals and vitamin supplements

some pasture grass in the summer months

The average North American cow can turn this much food into 6000 L (6340 quarts) of whole fresh milk a year — enough to keep you and 15 of your friends supplied with milk to drink all year. A super-cow could do a lot more. A Cuban cow, Urbe Blanca, set the record in 1982 for the highest milk yield in a single day. She produced 106.3 L (112 quarts) of milk.

Designer cows

Dairy cows today look pretty tame, but their ancestors were wild cattle that used to range the woods of northern Europe and parts of Asia. You can get an idea of what wild cattle looked like from the 17 000-year-old cave paintings of Lascaux in southwest France. (See illustration above.) The last of these animals, called aurochs or giant oxes, is said to have died in Poland in 1627.

A wild cow produced just enough milk each day to feed her one or two calves. But ever since cattle became domesticated more than 8000 years ago, people have wanted cows to produce more milk. In the past hundred years, scientists have discovered how characteristics are passed on from parents to children. Farmers have been able to use this new science of heredity, called genetics, to breed better milk-producing cows.

What cuts lawns and gives 100 glasses of milk a day?

A lawn moo-er.

How does genetics work in improving dairy animals? Think of your own family. If both your parents are tall, you will probably be taller than average, too. With dairy cattle, a good milk producer is likely to have daughters who are better-than-average milk producers. Over the years, farmers can improve their herds using selective breeding. They select high-producing cows and good bulls, or sires, to be parents for the new calves. Cows are selected as superior mothers on the basis of their milk production. Sires are selected as good fathers on the basis of the milk-producing abilities of their daughters.

Modern farmers often use computers to match up their cows with good sires. First the farmer asks a specialist to visit the herd and evaluate each cow. Then the

specialist uses a computer to search through the records of hundreds of bulls. At the end of the search, the computer prints out a list of a few of the bulls with traits suitable to complement the traits of the cow. When the sire is chosen, his frozen sperm is used for the artificial in-semination of the cow. In North America, more than half of all dairy cows have been bred by artificial insemination.

It's lucky that dairy animals don't have family reunions. Because, if they did, the owners of a bull named Bendalls Adema would be in trouble. By the time he died

in County Dublin, Ireland, he had sired an estimated 212 000 sons and daughters by artificial insemination.

The top five milk-producing countries are the Soviet Union in first place, then the United States, France, India and West Germany. These countries produce half the world's milk (including milk from other dairy animals, such as goats). Farmers in the United States, Canada and some Western European countries have been the most successful in improving their herds to make each cow more productive. This means they need fewer cows because each cow is such a good producer. North American cows are the superstars of milk production, and they are getting better all the time.

Test your dairy cow savvy

There are more than 160 million dairy cows in the world. More than 10 million of them live in the U.S., most in the top milk-producing states of Wisconsin, California, New York, Minnesota and Pennsylvania. Two million more cows live in Canada, with three-quarters of those on farms in Quebec and Ontario. North American dairy cows belong to one of seven breeds:

Jersey
Holstein-Friesian
Canadienne
Ayrshire
Dual-purpose Shorthorn
Guernsey
Swiss

Can you match each cow with the name of its breed? (Answers on page 80.)

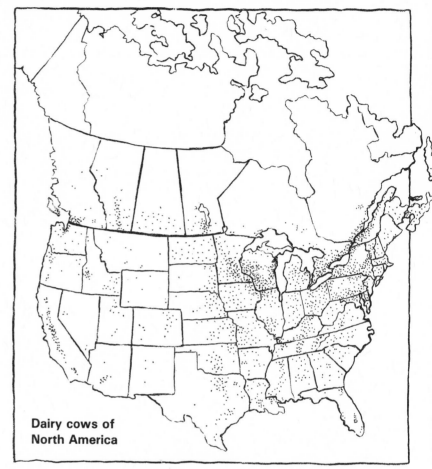

Dairy cows of North America

1. Red, roan, white or a mixture of red and white. I am a "dual purpose" animal, which means that I am raised for both milk and beef. That's why my body is heavier and more thick-set than breeds that are milk producers only. Who am I?

2. Fawn coloured or brown with some shading. My creamy-coloured milk contains 5.2% milk fat, which is richer than milk produced by any other breed. My name might remind you of a sweater but I am really named after the Channel Island where I originated. I am the smallest of the dairy breeds. Who am I?

3. Dark brown to silver grey. Some cows are nervous and sensitive, but not I. I am larger than most dairy breeds and very rugged — as you might expect when you learn that my breed developed in a rugged country in the mountains. Who am I?

4. Black or dark brown. I am the only breed of cow developed in Canada, and even to-day hardly any of my breed live outside Quebec. My ancestors crossed the ocean on ships from Normandy and Brittany to New France. Some may even have come with Jacques Cartier around 1541. I am known for my gentleness and my hardy constitu-tion. Who am I?

5. White and reddish brown. I don't like to sound vain, but I have been called the most beautiful of all the dairy breeds. I came originally from the hilly country of Ayr, Scotland, and I still can thrive in terrain that more wimpy cows find too rugged. Who am I?

6. Buff colour with distinctive white spots. My milk is often sold under the label of "golden" because of its golden colour. It is rich in milk fat, too — 4.8%. I also come from one of the Channel Islands, and I am noted for my quiet disposition. Who am I?

7. Black (or, less often, red) spots on a white background. In a popularity contest, I would win. There are more dairy cattle from my breed in the United States than any other. That's because I'm such a great milk producer and I'm getting better every year. My breed provides more than 90% of the milk in the U.S. I come from the Netherlands. Who am I?

Milk inventions

4.

Milk didn't always come chilled, in cartons and plastic bags from supermarket fridges. It came warm, straight from the cow. Read on to learn about some inventions that have made milk cold, safe and plentiful.

Hot milk

When milk comes from the cow, it is 35° C (95° F) — about the same as your own body temperature. In milk this warm, bacteria multiply very quickly. To slow down the growth of bacteria, milk needs to be quickly chilled and kept cool. In 1851, a Florida doctor, John Gorrie, patented a mechanical refrigeration system. But refrigeration wasn't used much for milk until the 1880s and later. Finally, milk could be kept longer and shipped in refrigerated railway cars greater distances from the cow. You didn't need your own back-yard cow any longer — you could buy milk from a farmer who lived far away.

Milk-spoiler test

If you want to see the difference refrigeration makes to milk, try this test. Pour 125 mL (½ cup) of milk into a cup and let it sit at room temperature. (Label it "milk experiment" so that no one will drink your milk or put it back into the refrigerator by mistake.) Pour another 125 mL (½ cup) of milk into another cup and leave it in the refrigerator. Every 12 hours or so, use the nose test. When the milk at room temperature is just beginning to smell slightly sour, look at it closely. Does it look any different? Try adding a bit of it to a cup of hot coffee or tea. You should see flecks of milk sitting on top of the coffee or tea. Bacteria have been souring the milk by turning milk sugar into lactic acid. This acid and the heat of the hot beverage cause the protein to clump together into a curd. Let the rest of the room-temperature milk sit for two to three days. It will thicken and clot.

Milk that spoils goes through several stages. At first, the milk looks the same, but invisible lactic acid bacteria are multiplying furiously. These bacteria turn lactose into lactic acid, which in turn curdles the casein protein. When enough lactic acid has formed, the acid eventually kills the lactic acid bacteria. Now organisms such as yeasts, moulds and other kinds of bacteria begin to grow.

After two or three days, the milk at room temperature has become decidedly less appealing. The milk left in the refrigerator should still be sweet and deliciously drinkable. Check the thermometer below to see how long milk keeps at different temperatures.

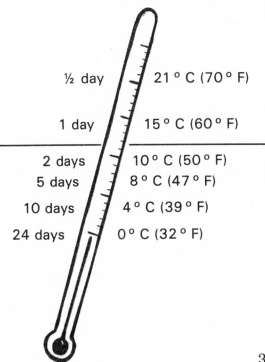

½ day	21° C (70° F)
1 day	15° C (60° F)
2 days	10° C (50° F)
5 days	8° C (47° F)
10 days	4° C (39° F)
24 days	0° C (32° F)

Safe milk

Every carton of milk you buy has Louis Pasteur's name on it: it's part of the word pasteurized. Why is Louis so lucky? Because he developed a process now called pasteurization, which has made milk safe to drink.

Surprisingly, Pasteur's famous scientific work that led to the development of pasteurization was not done with milk at all, but with wine and beer. Something was spoiling French wines and beer, making them sour. In 1856, Emperor Napoleon III called on Louis Pasteur, a well-known scientist, to save the French wine industry. Looking at samples of wines under a microscope, Pasteur discovered that the spoiled wine contained two different kinds of yeast. A useful one turned sugar into alcohol, which everyone wanted. The other turned alcohol into vinegar, which was undrinkable. Pasteur showed that the yeast organisms causing the spoilage were carried invisibly in the air all around us. And he showed how to rid the wine of the vinegar-producing yeasts. Since yeasts are living organisms, they can be killed by heat. The process of using controlled heat to kill organisms in food became known as pasteurization.

If pasteurization would work for wine, why not for milk, too? It turned out that heating milk to about 63° C (145° F) for 30 minutes kills the germs without destroying the flavour. Pasteurization solves two problems with milk: it kills the bacteria and yeasts that make milk go sour, and it makes milk safe to drink by destroying germs like typhoid and tuberculosis that used to kill people. Now all the cow's milk you drink has been pasteurized using a faster method of heating the milk to 72° C (161° F) for 16 seconds and cooling it immediately to 4° C (39° F).

Although now you can't buy raw (unpasteurized) milk, it took a while for pasteurization to catch on. By the 1890s, a few American dairies were starting to pasteurize milk. In 1908, J.J. Joubert Ltée in Montreal became the first dairy in the British empire to set up a pasteurizing plant and sell pasteurized milk in glass bottles.

What's the fastest food on earth?

Milk. It's "past-your-eyes" before you know it.

More milk

Calves get milk from their mothers by compressing the base of the teat between their tongue and upper gum and then relaxing the pressure. All milking machines now use a similar on-and-off pressure. But the first milking machine used a continuous vacuum. Invented in 1862 by L.O. Colvin, an American engineer, this machine had four rubber cups that fitted around the cow's teats. A vacuum sucked out the milk, which ran into a container. Unfortunately, continuous suction was painful for the cow. Later milking machines imitated the "open and close" action of the hand of an experienced milker. Milking machines were not used much until Gustav de Laval's "milker" appeared in 1918. Until then, hand milkers could still milk faster than machines.

Barn work-out

Some early milking machines worked on pedal power. Imagine milking a cow with your feet.

Creamed milk

The old way to separate cream from milk was to use gravity. Milk is an emulsion of fat globules dispersed throughout the milk. The fat globules are somewhat lighter than the rest of the milk. So if you let milk from the cow sit for 24 hours, the cream will rise to the top, where it can be skimmed off with a cream skimmer. The problem is that relying on gravity is slow, and letting the milk sit for 24 hours allows bacteria to multiply, which sours the milk.

Gustav de Laval of Sweden invented a cream separator in 1879 that could separate cream from milk in 13 minutes. His separator used centrifugal force. If you've ever taken a ride at a fair that spins you around quickly, you've

de Laval cream separator

experienced centrifugal force. In de Laval's separator, the lighter cream settled in the middle of the spinning container, while the heavier milk was flung to the outside and drained off. The first cream separators in North America were set up in 1882. By about 1930, most North American farmers used a separator on their farm to separate cream for sale to the creamery. Now they sell their milk whole to the dairy, to be separated there.

Lettuce centrifuge

You can compare the speed of gravity with centrifugal force when you prepare lettuce for salad. Wash the lettuce in a colander or strainer. Now use gravity to separate the water from the salad by leaving the colander of lettuce in the sink. Some of the water will drip through. Getting impatient? Then try the tea towel–fling method. Put the wet lettuce in a clean tea towel. Gather the ends of the tea towel together and whirl the tea towel round and round your head very quickly. (It's best to do this outside!) Be sure to hold on tight to the ends of the tea towel. Centrifugal force is the tug exerted on your hand as the

tea towel whirls and the water droplets fling outwards. You can buy plastic spin dryers for salad greens that work using centrifugal force.

Fat milk

What is more valuable the fatter it is? Milk. But until 1890, there was no accurate and simple way to tell how much fat was in milk. Then Dr. Stephen Babcock, an agricultural chemist from Wisconsin, invented a test so simple that it could be done right on the farm. You might say, "So what? Who cares how much fat is in milk?" Dairy farmers do, because the higher the fat content in their milk, the more they get paid for it. Once the Babcock test made it easy to measure the fat content of milk, farmers started to breed cows that would give lots of milk with a high fat content. So this simple test, which was used on farms until quite recently, was one of the inventions that made possible the genetic improvements that produced super-cows.

Try your own fat test

Your test won't be as accurate as the Babcock test, but you'll be able to tell which dairy product has the most milk fat.

You'll need:
   a large piece of uncoated brown paper
      (a paper grocery bag works well)
   samples of different kinds of milk products. You may not be able to get all of these, but use as many as you can:
      table cream
      skim milk
      homogenized or whole milk
      whipping cream
      sour cream
      whey (see "Make Miss Muffet's curds and whey" on page 18 for how to make whey)
      2% milk
      cereal cream (or half-and-half cream)
      butter

Put a drop from each of your milk-product samples onto the grocery bag paper. Label each drop, so that you can remember afterwards which one is which. Leave the brown paper alone for a while until the moisture from the samples has dried.

Compare the spots that are left. Do you notice any differences? Some of the spots will look greasier than others. Hold up the brown paper against a window when it is light outside. Which grease spots let the most light through? The more milk fat in the sample, the more light gets through. Turn to page 80 to find out the milk-fat content of the different samples.

5. Cow to carton

Did you know it takes about two to four days for milk to get from the cow to your refrigerator? During that time, the milk is not touched by human hands. The complicated process involves tanker trucks, huge refrigerators, pasteurizers and packagers. About 1700 dairy plants in the United States produce 23 billion litres (6 billion gallons) of milk a year. In Canada, 400 dairies process 4.7 billion litres (1.25 billion gallons). Here's how.

On the farm

1. Farmers milk their cows twice a day with milking machines. To make sure that everything is clean, they first wash the cow's udder and teats with a disinfectant solution and then rinse and dry them. The massaging action of cleaning

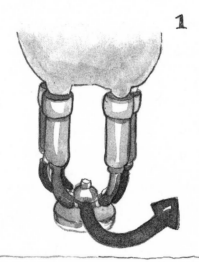

stimulates the flow of milk. Then the four rubber cups of the milking machine are attached to the cow's four teats. The milking machine gently squeezes and releases the teats to draw the milk out. It takes less than five minutes to milk a cow with a milking machine.

2. Milk from the teats flows through a tube into a receiver jar. The receiver jar stores the milk briefly until it is pumped into a big holding tank.

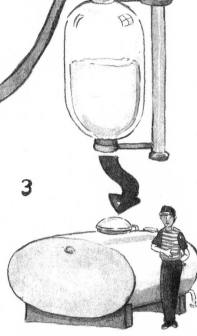

3. The milk in the holding tank must be cooled quickly to just below 4° C (39° F) — about the same temperature as your refrigerator — in order to stop bacteria from growing and spoiling the milk.

4. Every other day, a refrigerated, stainless steel dairy tank truck stops at the farm to collect the milk and take it to the dairy plant. The driver also collects samples of the milk in sterilized bottles, which she takes to a lab to be tested for protein, fat, lactose and water content as well as for impurities. Milk that contains pesticides, drugs like penicillin, or harmful bacteria is rejected, and the farmer who provided the contaminated milk may have to pay a heavy fine.

At the dairy

5. In the dairy plant, computer-controlled machines test the raw milk for milk-fat content, acidity, flavour, odour and bacterial count before the milk is pumped into a large, refrigerated storage tank. On its way to the storage tank, the milk goes through a **clarifier**, which removes any dust or hair that may have fallen into the milk.

6. Some of the milk from the tank goes through a separator that mechanically **separates** raw milk into skim milk and cream. The rest of the milk is **standardized** to bring it to a uniform milk-fat content. The standardizer automatically dilutes high-fat milk with skim milk and adds cream to low-fat milk.

7. Next the milk is **pasteurized** to kill bacteria that sour milk or make it unsafe to drink. During this process, milk is heated quickly to at least 72.8° C (161° F) for at least 16 seconds and then quickly cooled to 4° C (39° F).

8. Almost all milk is **homogenized** in a homogenizer, which forces milk under very high pressure through very small holes. This process breaks up the fat globules into particles ⅛ their former size. The protein coating that quickly forms around each fat particle keeps the particles from joining back up.

When the fat particles are that tiny, they stay evenly suspended. Before homogenization, milk fat used to rise to the top of the milk bottle. You had to shake your milk before you drank it. Homogenization also gives the milk a smoother, richer texture and a whiter colour than unhomogenized milk.

46

11. These containers are packed into cases and are stored briefly in a cold room at 1° C (34° F) before being put onto refrigerated trucks to be rushed to retail stores for you to buy. Milk can be kept on store shelves for up to a week. Before you buy milk, always check the "Best before" date on the container.

BEST BEFORE

9. Small amounts of vitamin D are added to the milk, which **fortifies** it.

10. Automatic machines package the cold milk in paper cartons, rigid plastic jugs or flexible plastic bags.

Recycle those cartons

Plastic milk containers should be returned to the store or added to your recycling bin. But cardboard milk cartons can be recycled in other ways, once you've drunk the milk inside. You can turn them into skyscrapers, boats, birdfeeders, mail boxes, candles, gift boxes and blocks. All you need are sharp strong scissors and lots of imagination. Don't forget to wash out your milk cartons and let them dry before you reuse them. If you want to paint your milk cartons, latex house paint covers milk cartons the best. On the next few pages you'll find some ideas to get you started on your milk carton crafts.

Holstein gift boxes

Here's an udderly new way to wrap gifts.

You'll need:
>   thick poster paint or latex paint —
>   black and white
>   a clean milk carton of a size that
>   matches the size of the gift
>   red ribbon

1. Paint your milk carton white.
2. When the white paint is thoroughly dry, paint on big black spots, just like the spots on a Holstein. Let the paint dry.
3. Open up the top of the carton and put your gift inside.
4. Close the carton. Make a hole through the ridge at the top of the carton. Tie a red ribbon through the hole to hold the carton shut.

This gift box needn't be thrown away once the gift is taken out. It can be used as a container for pencils.

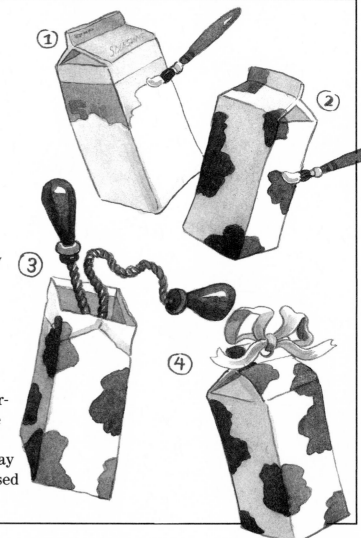

Milk containers

Goat's stomach   Arabs riding camels across the desert used to store milk in goat or sheep stomachs, or so we are told.

Milk cans used by farmers   British farmers used to sell their raw milk in these 77-L (17–Imperial gallon) cans. Now raw milk is collected from farms in refrigerated tank trucks.

Cardboard cartons   Milk was first sold in plastic-coated cardboard milk cartons in 1932. The carton protects the milk from ultraviolet light that may kill some of the milk's vitamins. Filling machines can fill about 250 cartons a minute.

Milk bottles   Milk bottles were first used in the 1880s. In 1884, Dr. Hervey Thatcher of Potsdam, New York, patented the first milk bottle, the "Thatcher milk protector." The "cream top" milk bottle became popular in the 1920s. Since milk was not yet homogenized, cream rose to the top and could be skimmed off. Now returnable glass milk bottles like these are found only in stores that sell collectors' items.

Plastic containers   Milk in plastic containers became available in 1964. Now Canadians prefer to buy their milk in packs of three 1-L bags, but Americans most often buy milk in 1-gallon jugs. Recyclers like these containers because the jugs can be returned and recycled and the plastic bags can be washed and reused.

Make a name for yourself!

You'll need:
    Milk Glue
    a squeeze bottle
    empty, clear plastic milk bags (washed
        and dried)
    food colouring
    wool or string

1. Make Milk Glue following the directions on page 19, with one important change. Use less water — only 25 mL (2 tbsp) so that your milk glue is quite thick.
2. Divide your glue into three portions, and use food colouring to dye each portion a different colour.

3. Put one of your coloured glue portions into a squeeze bottle (like the kind you squeeze mustard out of).

4. With the squeeze bottle, write your name on the clear plastic bag. When you run out of one colour of glue, fill your squeeze bottle with the next colour of glue and continue writing your name. Make sure that all the letters are firmly connected together.

5. Set the bag aside and let your name dry for at least 24 hours.
6. Peel your name off the bag and hang it on your door, using a piece of coloured wool or string.
7. If you have any of the glue mixture left over, don't throw it out. You can use it to make beads for a necklace.

Milk-carton boats

You can turn old milk cartons into a whole fleet of boats.

To make a **sailboat, you'll need:**
- scissors
- a milk carton (any size)
- a paper plate

1. Cut off one side of a carton.
2. Make slits in the opposite sides to hold a paper plate that you've trimmed into a rectangular sail.

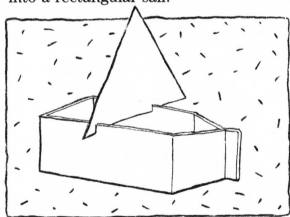

To make an **ocean liner**, you'll need:
- tape or glue
- a 2-L (2-quart) milk carton
- 2 250-mL (half-pint) cartons
- a cardboard tube (an empty paper towel or toilet paper roll)
- paint, straws, dental floss

1. Tape shut the opening of the milk carton and lay the carton flat on its side.
2. Tape or glue two smaller cartons together, upright and side by side, on top of the large carton.

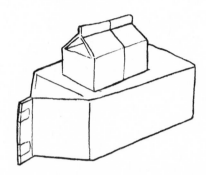

3. Cut two rings that are 5 cm (2 inches) long from the cardboard tube. Make two slits opposite each other in each tube. Fit the slits over the peaked ridges on the tops of the 250-mL (half-pint) cartons.
4. Paint on portholes. You can use striped straws and dental floss to create a railing around the top deck.

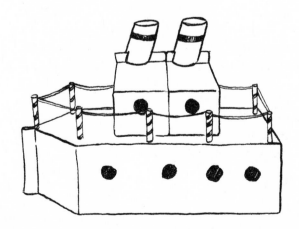

Make a Swiss cheese candle

Be sure to get an adult to help you with this craft.

You'll need:
- 1 500-g (1-lb) package of paraffin wax
- 1 796-mL (28-oz) tin can (empty and washed). Bend one side into a spout.
- a heavy pot
- old wax crayons (all of the same colour)
- a stick
- oven mitts
- scissors
- 1 1-L (1-quart) milk carton. You can make two shorter candles if you prefer by using two 500-mL (1-pint) milk cartons instead.
- cooking oil
- 1 candle that is as tall as the milk carton
- ice cubes, the smaller the better

1. Place the paraffin in the tin can.
2. Place the tin can inside the pot. Fill the pot with water as high as halfway up the tin can.

3. Place the pot on the stove on a low heat. **Be careful. Paraffin wax can catch fire very easily. And try not to breathe the vapours.**
4. When the paraffin wax has melted, add the crayons to the melted wax to provide colour.
5. When the crayons have melted, remove the pot from the heat and stir the wax with a stick. Use oven mitts to protect your hands.
6. Cut the peaked top off the carton.
7. Grease the inside of the milk carton with cooking oil.
8. Pour about half of the melted paraffin into the carton.
9. Press the candle into the centre of the paraffin so that its wick extends above the carton.
10. Fill the milk carton with ice cubes, encircling the candle.
11. Pour in the rest of the paraffin to the top of the carton, making sure that the wick is free.

12. When the paraffin has turned hard, peel off the milk carton. Do this over the sink, because water from the melted ice will drain off. Now you have a candle with more holes than Swiss cheese.

For the birds

Count how many different kinds of birds you can attract to eat from your milk-carton birdfeeder.

You'll need:
  scissors
  a 1-L (1-quart) milk carton
  a chopstick (or pencil or a piece of
    tree-twig about the size of a pencil)
  birdseed
  tape
  string

1. Cut a rectangular opening near the bottom of the milk carton as shown.
2. Push the chopstick right through the carton below the opening. This provides a perch for the bird to sit on while eating.

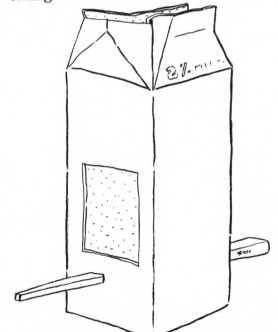

3. Put some birdseed in your feeder. Tape the top closed. Punch a hole through the carton at the top and suspend your birdfeeder from a tree branch as shown. Make sure that you put your birdfeeder in a place where it can't be sprung upon by cats or other enemies of birds.

6. Milk to go!

What else can you do with milk besides drink it? Eat it! About 65% of the milk produced in the United States and Canada is made into butter, cheese, ice cream, yogurt, skim-milk powder and other products. Only about 35% is drunk as milk and cream. You can make your own ice cream, yogurt and other milk treats. Read on to find out how.

What do you get when you cross a cow with an earthquake?

A milk shake.

A woman went up to the counter in a dairy bar. "I want a banana split for my little boy," she said. "I'm sorry," said the salesperson, "but we don't take trade-ins."

Anyone for fried milk?

If you lived in Spain, you'd love fried milk! Spanish children come home on a cold day to eat *leche frita*, which means fried milk. Here's how you can fry up some milk for dessert tonight.

You'll have to begin about three hours before dinner. Get your adult helper to give you a hand with some of the steps.

You'll need:
   a square glass cake pan
   a wooden spoon
   750 mL (3 cups) milk
   125 mL (½ cup) cornstarch
   90 mL (6 tbsp) sugar
   a pot
   a knife

1. Put the cake pan in the refrigerator so that it gets cold.
2. Mix the milk, cornstarch and sugar in the pot.
3. Cook over low heat for 10 to 15 minutes until very thick. Stir the whole time.
4. Pour the thickened mixture into the cold dish. Refrigerate for two hours.
5. Now your milk will be rubbery. Cut it into bite-size squares with a knife that you have first dipped into cold water.

The next step involves preparing the ingredients you need to cook your fried milk.

You'll need:
   1 egg
   3 bowls
   60 mL (¼ cup) milk
   a fork
   125 mL (½ cup) breadcrumbs
   5 mL (1 tsp) cinnamon
   125 mL (½ cup) sugar
   30 mL (2 tbsp) butter
   30 mL (2 tbsp) olive oil
   a frying pan
   an egg flipper

6. Break the egg into one bowl. Add the milk. Beat together with a fork.
7. Measure the breadcrumbs into the second bowl.
8. Mix the cinnamon and sugar together in the third bowl.
9. Melt the butter and oil together in the frying pan and put the frying pan on a burner turned on to medium heat.
10. Lift one of your bite-size squares of milk from the cake pan. Drop it gently into the beaten egg and milk, then into the breadcrumbs. Then lift it into the frying pan and fry on both sides until golden. The butter and oil will bubble.
11. Remove from pan, sprinkle with the cinnamon-sugar mixture, and serve hot.

Yogurt: a wonder food

Some people once thought yogurt was a wonder food. In 1950 Gayelord Hauser wrote an influential article claiming that yogurt was one of the world's five wonder foods. (If you don't like yogurt, you might want to check out one of the other four: brewer's yeast, powdered skim milk, wheat germ and blackstrap molasses.) After reading Hauser's article, many people tried out yogurt for the first time.

Dr. Elie Metchnikoff was another yogurt fan. He believed that yogurt was an elixir of life, and his opinions were taken seriously because he was a Nobel prize-winning scientist. His evidence? The large numbers of Bulgarians who managed to live to be 100. Metchnikoff decided they live so long because Bulgarians ate so much yogurt — some of them as much as 3 kg (7 lbs) of yogurt a day. He argued that friendly yogurt bacteria produced lactic acid that killed off harmful bacteria and thus cleansed the body of poisons. He was so convinced by his theory that he publicly announced that he would live to at least 100 by eating lots of yogurt. He died in 1916 at the age of 71.

What's pink and very dangerous?

Shark-infested strawberry yogurt.

Make your own yogurt

Yogurt is milk that has been curdled to a custardy consistency by bacteria. To make your own yogurt, you'll need a "starter culture." Your starter can be a few spoonfuls of fresh, plain, whole-milk yogurt bought at a grocery or health food store. Make sure that the yogurt contains a live, active culture and has not been pasteurized after fermentation. Don't use flavoured yogurt.

Your starter yogurt is called a culture because it contains the living organisms that digest the milk sugar and turn it into lactic acid. It is this action of the bacteria that sours the milk, curdles the milk protein and turns the milk into a tart, custardy treat — yogurt.

You'll need:
  625 mL (2½ cups) milk (You can use homogenized, 2%, skim milk or milk reconstituted from skim-milk powder.)
  a kitchen thermometer
  a pot made of stainless steel, glass or enamel
  a wooden spoon
  15 mL (1 tbsp) plain yogurt
  some wide-mouthed jars with screw-on lids
  a large flat cake pan
  a thick towel
You can adjust the proportions depending on how much yogurt you want to

make. Just make sure that you use 15 mL (1 tbsp) of yogurt for every 625 mL (2½ cups) of milk.

1. Kill any bacteria by putting the milk in the pot and heating it to 82° C (180° F) at a low heat on the stove. At this temperature, tiny bubbles will form around the edge of the pot. Check the temperature with a kitchen thermometer. (If a skin forms on top of the milk, the milk is too hot. Take the pot off the stove and remove the skin from the milk with a wooden spoon.)

2. As soon as the milk reaches 82° C (180° F), remove the pot from the stove and let the milk cool to 44-46° C (110-115° F). This cooling will take about half an hour at room temperature. You have to cool the milk before adding the yogurt starter, because yogurt is a living organism that will die above 49° C (120° F).

3. Add the yogurt culture to the cooled milk. Mix the yogurt thoroughly into the milk, using the wooden spoon.

4. Pour the mixture gently into the jars. Screw on the lids.

5. Incubate the mixture by keeping it at a constant temperature of 43° C (110° F). Remember that below 32° C (90° F), the yogurt bacteria will be alive but too cold to work; above 49° C (120° F) they will die. A good way to help the mixture stay at the right temperature is to put the jars containing the mixture into a pan of warm (not hot) water. The water in the outside container should be level with the yogurt mixture in the jars.

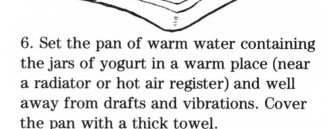

6. Set the pan of warm water containing the jars of yogurt in a warm place (near a radiator or hot air register) and well away from drafts and vibrations. Cover the pan with a thick towel.

7. Do not disturb! Leave the jars alone overnight (or about eight hours). The yogurt is ready if it pulls away in one piece from the sides of the jar when you tilt it. If it's not ready, leave it for two more hours and check again. But don't let it incubate too long or the yogurt will become very tart.

8. As soon as it's ready, store your yogurt in the refrigerator. After 12 hours or so in the refrigerator, your yogurt will be chilled and ready to eat. But don't eat all your yogurt! Remember to save some to start your next batch.

You can experiment with different kinds of milk when you make your yogurt. Try whole milk, 2%, skim, evaporated or powdered. Record the time that each takes to turn into yogurt and the taste of each batch. Keep a record of how many generations of yogurt you can grow from your original batch of starter.

Jazz it up

Jazz up your yogurt by adding one or more of the following: sliced fruit, jam, jelly, applesauce, honey, brown sugar. Or try the yummy yogurt recipes on this page.

Delicious drinks

Put 250 mL (1 cup) of yogurt, 500 mL (2 cups) of orange juice and a ripe banana into an electric blender. Blend for a minute, and presto! A nutritious drink for two people.

On a hot summer day, these drinks will cool you down:
Blend 250 mL (1 cup) of yogurt with 250 mL (1 cup) of water.

- For a Middle Eastern **laban**, stir into the yogurt-and-water mix a pinch of salt and two spoonfuls of chopped fresh or dried mint. Pour over ice cubes in a tall glass.
- For an Indian **lassi**, add to the yogurt-and-water mix 20 mL (1½ tbsp) of sugar or honey. For an unforgettable flavour, you can also stir in 1 mL (¼ tsp) of rose-water or orange-blossom water (available at a drugstore).

Yogurt popsicles

- Mix a package of your favourite flavoured jelly powder with a 1-kg (2-lb) tub of yogurt. Pour the mixture into popsicle moulds (or paper cups or ice-cube trays). Put the moulds in the freezer. When the popsicles start to freeze, put a popsicle stick into each one.
- Or you can mix a 355-mL (12-oz) can of frozen grape juice or orange juice with 1 kg (2 lbs) of yogurt. Don't dilute the juice first. Then pour into moulds, start to freeze and add popsicle sticks.

Say cheese

Cheese is actually just milk, with much of its water and lactose and some of its minerals removed. An average cheese is two parts protein, three parts fat and three parts water, plus some calcium. Before the days of refrigeration, cheese was very important as a source of protein throughout the whole year. Milk produced from rich summer pasture grass could be turned into cheese and eaten in the winter, when food was scarce. North Americans nowadays eat almost a third of their milk in the form of cheese.

No one knows for certain who invented cheese, but according to one story it was an Arab. He had to make a trip across the desert on his camel. He took along some fresh milk, stored in a pouch made from a lamb's stomach. Feeling hot and thirsty, he took a drink of milk. Surprise! It tasted good, but it wasn't milk any more. The milk had separated into thick white clumps and some thin, bluish, watery liquid — curds and whey.

This legendary camel ride combined four elements needed for making cheese. First there was the milk. Then the bumpy camel ride over the sand-dunes provided a churning motion. The desert provided heat, and the lamb's stomach provided rennin — an enzyme that helps lambs digest milk by making it curdle.

Cheese Talk

SAY CHEESE

THE BIG CHEESE

CHEESE IT! THE COPS

CHEESED OFF

CHEESE CAKE

60

How cheese is made

Large automated, computerized factories make most of our cheese, but the cheese-making process is easier to follow in a small operation like the one you see here. These cheesemakers are making Cheddar cheese. There are lots of different cheeses, but most cheesemakers go through the same basic steps.

1. Preparing the milk

Cheesemakers use pasteurized milk, unless the cheese is to be aged for 60 days or more. (The aging process kills germs, making pasteurization unnecessary.) To be pasteurized, the milk is poured into a big cheese vat and heated.

2. Adding a starter, rennet and colour

Since pasteurization kills the natural bacteria in milk, the cheese-maker adds a starter of lactic acid bacteria to help make the curds firm and improve the flavour of the cheese. Next, rennet is added and mixed thoroughly into the milk. This enzyme makes the protein particles clump together or coagulate. Sometimes a vegetable dye is also added. The mixture is left alone to give the rennet time to work its separation trick of dividing curds from whey.

What do you do with cheddar cheese when it's a year old?

Sing "Happy Birthday to you!"

3. Cutting the curd

Cheesemakers use big wire knives to cut the coagulated curd into small pieces. This process of "breaking the curds" helps separate the curds and drain off the whey. To speed up the separation process, the curds and whey are heated to a controlled temperature. Cheddars are heated to about 38° C (100° F) — the temperature of a very, very hot summer day. Some cheeses, called "cooked" cheeses (such as Swiss cheese), are heated to more than 53° C (128° F).

4. Draining off the whey

The whey is drained from the vat. But it's not thrown away. It's saved for feeding animals or to be used as an ingredient in some human foods such as cookies or ice cream. The curd is left alone till it mats together into a solid mass.

5. Salting the curd

Salt is added to help get rid of more whey, to improve the keeping quality of the cheese, and to make the cheese taste better. Sometimes salt is mixed directly into the curd in the cheese vat, and sometimes the cheese gets salted after it is pressed.

6. Pressing and curing the cheese

Cheesemakers cut the matted curd into blocks. The blocks are cut into small pieces and are packed into containers or cheesecloths, ready for pressing. The pressing removes more of the whey. If salt hasn't already been added, the cheeses are put in a salty bath and left there for a few days.

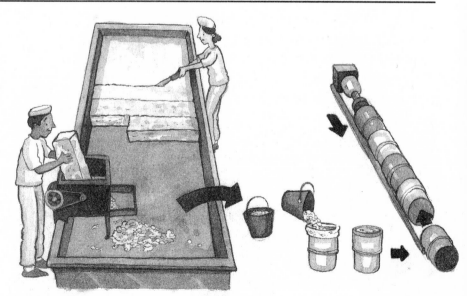

7. Ripening and packaging the cheese

Most cheese isn't eaten right away but is cured or aged in a cool, well-ventilated place for some months. During this ripening process, cheeses develop their characteristic flavours and textures. Some, such as Gruyère, develop holes, while cheddar acquires a sharper taste and Camembert a surface rind. Cheesemakers next cut and package the cheeses for market. Some cheeses, such as Edam and Gouda, are covered in a wax or plastic coating, which prevents unwanted moulds from getting into the cheese.

Make some cottage cheese

When you made Miss Muffet's curds and whey (see instructions on page 18), you were going through the first steps of making cottage cheese. Some people call this pot cheese, because you make it in a pot. Try turning your curds and whey into cheese.

You'll need:
a sieve or colander
cheesecloth (a piece of well-worn
    but clean gauze diaper will also
    work)
curds and whey (see page 18)
a bowl
some salt
some cream

1. Line a sieve or colander with a double thickness of cheesecloth.

2. When the curdling has stopped (step 3 on page 18), pour the curds and whey into the cheesecloth-lined sieve.
3. Gather together the corners of the cheesecloth and twist to form a bag containing the curds. Keep twisting to gently squeeze out as much whey as you can.
4. Put the curds into a bowl. Add a sprinkle of salt to taste and enough cream to moisten. Stir well. You now have creamed cottage cheese.
5. Refrigerate the cottage cheese. It will keep for almost a week, but it's best if you eat it right away.

Cheesey questions

How many kinds of cheese are there?

There are more than 400 kinds of cheese, each with its own special look, texture and taste. There's so much variety because cheeses are made from different kinds of milk using somewhat different methods. Many cheeses are made from cow's milk, but some are made of buffalo's milk, sheep's milk or goat's milk. The more whey that is pressed out during the pressing stage, the harder the cheese. A hard cheese, such as the Parmesan you grate and sprinkle on your spaghetti, has less than one-third water, while a soft cheese like Camembert is more than half water. Some cheeses are aged longer than others to develop a strong full-bodied flavour. Mild Cheddar cheese is only about two or three months old; nippy Cheddar is more than six months old. Some cheeses get their distinctive flavours from moulds or smoke or added flavourings such as caraway seeds.

Who eats the most cheese?

Contrary to what you might think, mice are not big cheese eaters. They'll eat cheese, but really much prefer a lemon gumdrop. French people eat the most cheese in the world. Each person in France on average eats about 19.5 kg (43 lbs) of cheese a year — almost double the amount eaten by North Americans.

What makes some cheeses blue?

A penicillium mould gives the nippy taste and blue veined appearance to cheeses like blue cheese, Stilton, Gorgonzola and Roquefort. The famous blue Roquefort cheeses have been made for more than 1200 years using a special method. They are made from sheep's milk and matured in lime-stone caves. Cheesemakers used to rely on the moulds growing on the cave walls to fall onto the cheese. These days they leave nothing to chance: they add carefully-measured amounts of mould to the curds to guarantee that each cheese is blue-veined.

Why are so many cheeses yellow or orange?

Cheeses made from cow's milk are usually yellow. The yellow is caused by carotene, a yellow or orange pigment in the grass and hay that cows eat. (Carotene is also what gives carrots and banana skins their colour.) The carotene from the cow's grassy diet gets into the milk fat and dyes the cheese yellow — it makes butter yellow, too. In winter, when cows don't eat fresh grass, they don't get this carotene colouring in their milk. Cheesemakers usually add a natural food colour to the milk so that the appearance of their cheese stays the same throughout the year. Cheeses and butter made from goat's milk are white because goats digest carotene so thoroughly that it doesn't colour their milk.

What makes cheese holey?

It looks as if a mouse has been nibbling your Swiss cheese, but it's really bacteria added specially to make the holes. Bacteria added during the cheesemaking process produce bubbles of carbon dioxide gas. This gas gets trapped in the cheese, making the holes or "eyes."

The big cheese

- Some people just don't know when to stop. In 1892, cheesemakers in Perth, Ontario, produced the largest round cheese the world had ever seen. The "Canadian Mite" weighted 9980 kg (22 000 lbs) and was made from the equivalent of one day's milk from 10 000 cows. This mammoth cheese was taken to the Chicago World's Fair of 1893 where it accumulated 10 000 autographs.

- According to the *Guinness Book of World Records*, Simon's Specialty Shop in Little Chute, Wisconsin, set the record for the largest cheese in 1988. It weighed 18 171 kg (40 060 lbs) and was taken on tour in a specially designed, refrigerated "Cheesemobile."

- James McIntyre was so impressed by another big cheese produced in Ingersoll, Ontario, in 1866 that he wrote his famous "Ode on the Mammoth Cheese." This celebration of Ingersoll's 3200-kg (7000-lb) cheese was reprinted in William Arthur Deacon's book *The Four Jameses: Canada's Four Worst and Funniest Poets* (1927):

> We have seen thee, queen of cheese,
> Lying quietly at your ease,
> Gently fanned by evening breeze
> Thy fair form no fly dare seize.

. . . .

> We'rt thou suspended from balloon,
> You'd cast a shade even at noon,
> Folks would think it was the moon
> About to fall and crush them soon.

Buttering up

How can you tell if your friend likes butter? By putting a buttercup under her chin to see if her skin looks yellowish — or so they say. Read on to find out more about butter and how to make your own.

Make some butter

It takes 21 kg (46 lbs) of milk to make 1 kg (2.2 lbs) of butter. If you want to make a lot of butter, it helps to have a butter churn. But you can easily make a bit of butter this way.

You'll need:
    250 mL (1 cup) of whipping cream at room temperature
    a small jar with a secure lid
    a bowl
    a wooden spoon

1. Pour the whipping cream into the jar.
2. Screw on the lid and shake vigorously. You'll notice after about ten minutes that your cream has separated into a bluish-white liquid (buttermilk) and pale yellow clumps of fat (butter).
3. Pour the butter and buttermilk into a bowl.
4. Pour off the buttermilk.
5. Wash the butter with cold water.

6. Press the butter against the side of the bowl with a wooden spoon and rinse with water until the water is clear. Make sure that all excess water is worked out — otherwise your butter will be "leaky."

Taste the butter. Does it look and taste just like the butter you buy at the store? Work a little salt into your butter and taste it again.

You can easily tell the difference between unsalted and salted butter. But did you know that professional butter tasters have to be able to tell the difference between 50 different kinds and qualities of butter? They classify defective butter as "crumbly," "sticky" or "leaky."

How does it work?
What happened to make the cream turn into butter? Butter is the particles of milk fat stuck together and separated from the buttermilk. Each fat globule in cream is wrapped in a membrane or coating. When you shake the cream, you break the membrane, allowing the particles of fat to stick together in larger and larger clusters.

Making the grade

Did you know that butter gets a report card? Butter has to pass an examination and is graded out of 100. This is what a report card would look like for perfect butter:

Flavour	45
Texture	15
Distribution of the water	10
Colour	10
State of the salt	10
Wrapping	10

Years ago, butter was shaped into nice round balls, using wooden paddles. It was often "printed" as well. A cylinder or cube of wood that had a special design carved into it was pressed into the block of butter, imprinting it with a pattern.

Other uses for butter

- Rub it into your hair to make your hair glossy. The ancient Greeks and Romans did this.

- Use it as a medicine. The ancient Egyptians used butter as a remedy for sore eyes.

- Use it as a skin cream. The women of ancient Rome used butter to make their skin smooth and satiny.

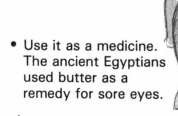

- Burn it. Until the 19th century, the Scots used butter in their oil lamps for light, just like the Inuit used blubber oil.

One thing you should never do with butter is rub it on burns. Put cold water on a burn, not butter; butter may cause infection in the burn.

The margarine wars

The very first synthetic food has been around for more than 100 years — margarine. Napoleon III of France hoped that, since cows could produce milk fat naturally, people might do it artificially. He sponsored a contest to create a cheap butter substitute to supply his army and navy. The winner, Hippolyte Mege-Mouriez, patented his invention in 1869. He called it oleo-margarine — "oleo" meaning beef fat and "margarine" after the Greek word, *margarites*, for pearl (because of margarine's pearly-white colour). His winning recipe was liquefied beef fat mixed with equal quantities of milk and water, plus a mystery ingredient — cow's udder, chopped up very fine. When the demand for margarine became greater than the supply of beef fat, vegetable oils were used instead of the animal fat.

Ice cream: the royal dessert

Once upon a time, kings and queens and emperors were almost the only people who could get ice cream to eat. In hot climates, chilled desserts were made with snow or ice that was rushed from mountain tops or packed away each winter in icehouses. The Roman emperor Nero used to eat a cool treat made from snow, honey and fruit juices — but no milk or cream. In 1295, Marco Polo came back to Italy from China with a recipe for a frozen sherbet-like dessert. Ices and sherbets soon took Europe by storm. At the wedding of Catherine de Medici and the future King Henry II of France in 1533, guests were served a different flavoured ice dessert every day for 34 days. Ice cream still cost a lot in 1790, when George Washington spent $200 in two months on ice cream. That would be thousands of dollars today.

That may seem to be an expensive treat, especially when you consider that almost half of ice cream is air. Without the air beaten into it, ice cream would be more like a frozen popsicle. Too much air makes the ice cream fluffy.

The other ingredients in ice cream are sugar, cream, whole milk and non-fat milk solids, egg yolks or whole eggs, flavouring and a stabilizer that prevents ice crystals from forming when the ice cream changes temperature. The cheaper the ice cream you buy, the more extra ingredients you get — artificial substitutes for cream, eggs and flavouring. Take a look at the list of ingredients on the ice-cream container the next time you take a scoop.

Vanilla is still by far the most popular flavour of ice cream, followed by chocolate and strawberry. But ice-cream companies have developed more than 400 other different flavours. Anyone for brandied apricot almond? Jelly bean? Pumpkin licorice? Grape noodle? Oat-bran jamoka?

If there were prizes for ice-cream eating, Alaskans would win. On average, they each eat 22 L (6 gallons) a year.

What's cold and pink and goes click, click?

A ball-point strawberry ice-cream cone.

The big scoop

A waffle maker invented the ice-cream cone at the Louisiana Purchase Exhibition in St. Louis in 1904. He noticed that the ice-cream stand nearby had run out of dishes to sell ice cream in. So he rolled one of his waffles into a cone, let it cool and filled it with ice cream. "The World's Fair Cornucopia" was born and became a great hit with fair-goers. Inventors soon were competing with each other to design the perfect ice-cream cone. There were spiral cones, cones that would stand up on the table, "dripless" cones with a built-in catch basin made of candy and cones with extra pouches for double or triple scoops. Environmentalists love the ice-cream cone, too, because it doesn't create litter and waste.

Make your own ice cream

You'll need at least two people for this — and a lot of muscle! The yummy treat you'll end up with is worth the effort.

You'll need:
a 500-mL (1-pint) carton of whipping cream
75 mL (⅓ cup) of sugar
a pinch of table salt
5 mL (1 tsp) of vanilla
a clean coffee can with a plastic lid
a wooden spoon (It's best to use one with a hole in it.)
ice (Crushed ice works best. Or use snow if it's winter.)
an ice bucket (or plastic pail)
rock salt (Rock salt, which you buy at a hardware store, works best, but table salt will do.)

1. Pour the whipping cream, sugar, table salt and vanilla into the coffee can and mix them together.

2. Punch a hole in the lid of the coffee can.

3. Push the handle of the wooden spoon through the lid. Then fit the lid on the can. The spoon is your "dasher."

4. Put a layer of ice on the bottom of the ice bucket or pail. Sprinkle the ice with 65 mL (¼ cup) of rock salt.

5. Put the coffee can on top of the ice in the pail. Put layers of rock salt and ice around the coffee can until the ice-and-salt mixture reaches the top. But don't use too much salt or your ice cream will be grainy. Use 3 parts ice to 1 part salt. Let the whole thing sit for three minutes.

6. Now for the hard part! Twirl the spoon handle (dasher) fast in your hands. At the same time, turn the coffee can around. You'll need four hands for this. It will take at least 20 minutes for the cream to freeze into ice cream. Take turns with your helper — when you get tired twirling the dasher, you can turn the coffee can. You'll know when the ice cream is freezing because it will get harder to turn the dasher.

7. When your ice cream is firm, take out the coffee can. Remove the dasher and put the lid back on. Put the can of ice cream in your freezer for at least one hour. Now taste your ice cream. It should be smooth and delicious.

8. If you like, stir sliced strawberries into the ice cream before you put it into the freezer.

How does it work?

That work you did turning the dasher made your ice cream smooth by adding air and keeping large ice crystals from forming. The smoothest ice cream has tiny air bubbles and tiny ice crystals. Did you notice that you had twice as much ice cream in the can as when you started? That's how much air your dasher has beaten into the cream.

Why salt the ice? Ice cream freezes at -3° C (27° F), but ordinary ice starts to melt at 0° C (32° F). If the tub contained just ice by itself, it would soon melt to an ice-water mixture and the ice cream wouldn't freeze. You need to lower the point at which ice starts to melt. That's where the salt comes in. Salt lowers the freezing point of water. Mixing salt with ice makes a substance with a freezing point of about -5° C (23° F), and that's cold enough to freeze the ice cream.

Ice-cream delights

Milk shakes (vanilla, chocolate or strawberry)

You'll need:
- 2 scoops of vanilla ice cream
- an electric blender (or a large jar with a screw-on lid)
- 500 mL (2 cups) of milk
- 5 mL (1 tsp) of vanilla for flavouring; or a few squirts of chocolate syrup; or some fresh strawberries

1. Put the ice cream in the blender or jar first and then pour in the milk. That way you'll avoid splashes.
2. Add your favourite flavouring.
3. Blend or shake for one minute.
4. Pour into a tall glass, add a straw and enjoy!

Make your milk shake extra-special. (But it will take practice.) After you have filled the glasses, try balancing a scoop of ice cream on the rim of the glass.

Igloos (makes 6)

If you put ice cream in a hot oven, it will melt, right? Not if it's insulated! Here's an ice-cream dessert that won't melt in the heat, because the ice cream is kept away from the heat by a thick blanket of fluffy meringue before it's baked. Some people call this dessert Baked Alaska. We're calling it Igloos because you will end up with six igloo-shaped mounds.

You'll need:
- 3 oranges, cut in half, with the orange scooped out so that you end up with an unbroken rind "basket." Cut a very thin slice off the bottom of each half orange, so that the basket sits up straight.
- 6 balls of ice cream (any flavour — chocolate tastes good with orange)
- meringue (instructions to follow)
- a cookie sheet

To make meringue, you'll need:
- an electric mixer and a bowl
- a spoon
- a rubber scraper
- 6 egg whites (get your adult helper to help separate the eggs)
- 1 mL (¼ tsp) salt
- 2 mL (½ tsp) cream of tartar
- 175 mL (¾ cup) sugar
- 5 mL (1 tsp) vanilla

1. Beat the egg whites until frothy.
2. Add the salt and cream of tartar and beat until stiff.
3. Beat in the sugar, a little at a time.
4. Beat in the vanilla.
Your meringue should now stand up in stiff, curly peaks.

To make your igloos:
1. Preheat your oven to 260° C (500° F).
2. Place your six orange halves on a cookie sheet.
3. Drop the balls of ice cream into the orange baskets.

4. Completely cover the ice cream and the orange in meringue.

5. Put the cookie sheet in the oven for no more than three minutes — or just until the meringue starts to get a little brown.
6. Serve at once. You'll surprise everyone when they discover that underneath that hot meringue, the ice cream is still frozen.

How does it work?
When you beat the egg whites to make the meringue, you trapped a lot of air bubbles. Those trapped air bubbles in the meringue are poor conductors of heat. The meringue insulates the ice cream from the heat of the oven, the same way that a picnic cooler, made of air-filled Styrofoam, keeps the cold drinks inside cold at the hot beach.

Milk by any other name

What do people call milk in other languages?

Dutch: melk

Italian: latte

French: lait

German: milch

Greek: galakt

Icelandic: mjólka

Portuguese: leite

Spanish: leche

Russian: moloko

Malay: soesoe

Arabic: laban

Chinese: nai

Bohemian: mleko

Romanian: lapte

The name Lebanon comes from the Arabic word for milk.

How many glasses of cold milk can you drink on an empty stomach?

Only one. After that, your stomach's not empty.

Glossary

Artificial insemination A process in breeding animals in which sperm is collected from a superior male, kept frozen until needed and then used to fertilize a female.

Bacteria Very tiny germs that can be seen only with a microscope. Some cause illness and others cause milk to sour.

Bacterial culture A concentration of one or more bacteria that is deliberately added to milk or cream to produce lactic acid or to give a desired flavour. Sometimes called a starter or starter culture.

"Best before" The date you find stamped on containers of perishable food such as milk and yogurt. This date is the latest at which the food can be sold at its best.

Casein One of the two kinds of milk protein, making up 80% of the protein in milk.

Centrifugal force When something is spinning around quickly in a circle, two equal and opposite forces are in balance: the centrifugal or "centre-fleeing" force and the centripetal or "centre-seeking" force. Centrifugal force can be used to separate skim milk from cream because the two substances have different densities (cream is lighter).

Clarification Milk-processing plants clarify milk by using centrifugal force to remove particles such as dust and other debris from milk.

Coagulation Tiny particles dispersed in a liquid clump together to form a solid mass.

Colostrum The name for the milk produced by mammal mothers in the first few days after they give birth. It is thicker than regular milk and contains substances that help the babies fight infections that would otherwise make them sick.

Creamery A factory where cream is churned into butter. Nowadays most creameries have been replaced by integrated milk-processing plants.

Curd The white solid that is produced in the cheesemaking process when milk is coagulated.

Dairy products Products that are made from milk, such as butter, cheese, yogurt, sour cream, chocolate milk, evaporated milk and skim-milk powder.

Emulsion A mixture in which fine particles of one liquid are evenly distributed in another liquid. Milk is an oil-in-water emulsion; butter is a water-in-oil emulsion.

Enzyme A substance produced by living cells that speeds up a chemical reaction but does not itself change. Some enzymes, such as lactase, help animals digest food.

Fermentation A process in which a living organism turns sugars into other chemical substances such as lactic acid when milk is fermented (or into alcohol when fruit juices are fermented).

Fermented milk Whole or skim milk that is curdled to a custardy consistency by bacteria that turn lactose into lactic acid.

Fluid milk Milk that is sold in stores in the form of milk or cream. Fluid milk is different from manufacturing milk, which gets turned into various products such as butter, cheese, ice cream, yogurt, casein and whey powder.

Heifer The name for a young female calf before she is bred and becomes a mother.

Homogenization   The process of breaking up fat globules into smaller ones. When milk is homogenized, the fat stays evenly distributed throughout the liquid and does not separate out and rise to the top.

Kumiss   A fermented, mildly alcoholic drink made in southeastern Russia from mare's milk. Kumiss looks like milk but bubbles and foams like beer.

Lactase   An enzyme secreted in the intestine that is needed to digest lactose.

Lactic acid   An acid that is produced from lactose by the action of lactic acid bacteria.

Lactose   A sugar that is found only in milk, just as fructose is a sugar found only in fruit.

Lactose intolerant   What we call people who are unable to digest milk sugar because their bodies do not produce enough lactase. These people feel sick when they consume milk.

Mammal   The only class of animal that produces milk to feed their babies in contrast to other classes such as birds, fish, reptiles or insects.

Mammary glands   Glands that mammals have to produce milk for their babies. Called udders in cows.

Milk solids   This is the 13% of milk that is left over after the water is removed.

Milk fat   Sometimes called butterfat. This is the fat in milk that you find in concentrated form in cream and butter. Sometimes abbreviated as M.F.

Non-fat solids   What is left of milk after the water and fat are removed. Skim-milk powder is a familiar example of non-fat solids.

Pasteurization   A process that uses controlled heat to kill harmful bacteria. This makes milk safe to drink and improves its keeping quality.

Raw milk   Milk from the dairy animal before it has undergone processing and pasteurization.

Rennin   An enzyme secreted in the fourth stomach of a nursing calf, sheep or goat. When extracted from the calves' stomachs and concentrated, it is called rennet and is used commercially in cheesemaking to make milk coagulate.

Ruminants   Hooved animals that chew their cud, such as cows, sheep, goats, antelopes and camels.

Selective breeding   A way of producing offspring with certain desired qualities, such as high milk production, by choosing animals with that quality to become parents.

Separator   A machine that uses centrifugal force to separate cream quickly from the rest of the milk.

Shelf life   The length of time that a food product will keep before its quality begins to deteriorate.

Teat   The nipple on a mammary gland that the baby animal sucks on to get milk.

Udder   The mammary gland of cows and some other animals.

Whey   The watery part of the milk that is left over when the curds have been removed.

Whey protein   Makes up 20% of the protein in milk. The rest is casein.

Yeast   Living one-celled organisms. Yogurt-making yeasts are used commercially to make yogurt. (Bakers use a different kind of yeast to make bread rise.)

Index

Answers

Test your dairy cow savvy, p. 36

1. The Dual-purpose Shorthorn
2. The Jersey
3. The Swiss
4. The Canadienne
5. The Ayrshire
6. The Guernsey
7. The Holstein-Friesian

Try your own fat test, page 43

whey — almost no milk fat
skim milk — 0.1% milk fat
2% milk — 2% milk fat
whole milk — 3.25% milk fat
cereal cream or half-and-half cream — 10% milk fat
sour cream — 14% milk fat
table cream — 18% milk fat
whipping cream — 35% milk fat
butter — 80% milk fat